Comprehend It!

Weird and Mysterious

Bruce Tuffin and Diane Henderson

World Teachers Press®

Published with the permission of R.I.C. Publications Pty. Ltd.

Copyright © 1999 by Didax, Inc., Rowley, MA 01969. All rights reserved.

First published by R.I.C. Publications Pty. Ltd., Perth, Western Australia.

Limited reproduction permission: The publisher grants permission to individual teachers who have purchased this book to reproduce the blackline masters as needed for use with their own students. Reproduction for an entire school or school district or for commercial use is prohibited.

Printed in the United States of America.

Order Number 2-5092
ISBN 1-58324-014-4

B C D E F   01 02

395 Main Street
Rowley, MA 01969

Comprehend It!

FOREWORD

The *Comprehend It!* series of blackline masters has been developed to improve student comprehension abilities at every level. The attractive format uses interesting writing, both fiction and nonfiction. The artwork is designed to be visually appealing, engaging students while assisting them in their understanding of the written material.

The book *Weird and Mysterious* has been written specifically for grades six through eight and although it is thematic, the theme is broad to allow integration into a whole-language program.

To assist you, while remaining unobtrusive to students, the comprehension exercises on each worksheet have been coded, using the following code:

> A = Literal
> B = Interpretative
> C = Evaluative

While some syllabuses do in fact promote four levels of comprehension, it is the authors' contention that the two final categories under this system may be quite happily placed together as Evaluative.

CONTENTS

Teacher Information .... 4 – 5

A Strange Triangle .... 6 – 8
Atlantis—Lost or Found? .... 9 – 11
Cycle .... 12 – 14
Batteries Included .... 15 – 17
"I Want To Drink Your Blood…" .... 18 – 20
They Just Disappeared .... 21 – 23
Premonition .... 24 – 26
A Helping Hand .... 27 – 29
Are We the First? .... 30 – 32
Tunguska .... 33 – 35
Asking Directions .... 36 – 38
Answers 39

| Comprehend It! | **Teacher Information** |

Introduction

Comprehension is an important part of any language program. While many students have the ability to read, their comprehension may not be fully developed. This series of blackline masters addresses comprehension at three levels, and provides high-interest, original fiction and nonfiction to improve comprehension abilities at every level.

The comprehension questions which follow each piece of writing fall into three main categories:

- literal
- interpretative
- evaluative

The activities are spread over three pages to allow you to provide appropriate levels of challenge to each student in your classroom. The breadth of these activities will challenge the brightest student, while allowing less capable students to work with the text and questions at their own level.

The answers to the literal-type questions have been provided for you, while answers to the interpretative and evaluative questions have not been included. These answers will vary according to each student's interpretation, understanding and personal knowledge. Answers to interpretative and evaluative questions will reflect both the included text as well as outside sources.

Levels of Comprehension

Modern approaches to teaching comprehension recognize the need for students to be able to comprehend more than in a literal form, and now look to develop the students' abilities to make inferences from the text, and then to also form opinions based upon their reading. The main levels of comprehension are explained below:

- **Literal:**
  These questions require a specific answer where all information is provided in the text. Students' responses are either correct or incorrect in accordance with the text. This level of questioning does not allow students to write any other answer than that found directly in the text.

- **Interpretive:**
  These types of questions require inferences to be made based on partial information provided in the text. Students are required to draw on information within the text and their own background knowledge of the topic. This level of questioning allows for a little more freedom as part of the answer relies on the student's understanding of the topic.

- **Evaluative:**
  Questions at this level require the student to make a judgement based on information in the text and his or her own opinions. They also require students to show an understanding and appreciation of the author's intent and any messages that may be contained. Good answers to these questions are broad. Their value lies in the student's ability to support his/her answer with both material from the text provided, as well as outside sources.

| Comprehend It! | **Teacher Information – Example Lesson Development** |

The following is a lesson development using one of the topics in this book.
It is an example of how the activity could be introduced, developed and extended.

Activity

A Strange Triangle: pages 6 to 8

Introductory Work

As with most reading activities, students will actively participate if they are motivated by the topic they are reading. As a result, the topics in this book have been selected for their interest levels. In addition, you can motivate students by introducing and talking about the idea of *A Strange Triangle*, and supporting this discussion with pictures. You will also need to provide students with strategies to handle the tasks involved. These include reading the passage several times, interspersed with reading the questions, so when the student begins answering the questions he/she has a good understanding of the text and the questions. Students should also be encouraged to explain their answers where required.

Completing the Worksheets

The following is a suggestion for the development of this activity.

1. Students read through the passage, individually, in pairs, or as a class.

2. Read the questions, so students understand what is required.

3. Students read the passage again with the questions in mind.

4. Students answer questions and write the answers in spaces provided. Ask the students to provide as much detail as they can to explain and justify their answers.

5. Answer the questions as a group or individually. Discuss reasons for correct and incorrect answers.

6. Discuss with the whole class any problem questions and also how there can be more than one correct answer to some questions.

Extension

The extension of this activity can occur in two main directions.

1. Follow the topic into other subject areas and allow it to develop into an across-the-curriculum theme.

2. Continue the activities in this book to further develop comprehension skills.

A STRANGE TRIANGLE

Most people have heard of the Bermuda Triangle, but not many know exactly where it is. Have a look at a map of the USA. Draw a line from Miami (Florida) east to Puerto Rico, then north to Bermuda and back to Miami. Now you have, roughly, the Bermuda Triangle.

What makes the Triangle so special? Well, there seems to be an awful lot of strange things happening there; things for which we have no natural explanation. And it's not just recently this has been happening either, although the area has received more publicity in the last twenty or so years.

So, just what happens in the Triangle that is so weird? Quite a lot of things! For example, compasses often go crazy, spinning round or even pointing in the wrong direction altogether. Christopher Columbus noticed this 500 years ago! It is still reported by ships and even aircraft today. Luckily, modern navigation doesn't rely on magnetic compasses any more!

There also seems to be something that can affect time in the Triangle. There have been stories of light aircraft, for example, flying into strange fogs. When they came out the other side, after just a few minutes flying time to them, it was to find that they had been gone for several hours! There's also the pilot who got lost. A control tower directed the plane to an airfield on a nearby island. The people on the island could see the plane circling overhead—but the pilot couldn't see them, or the buildings, or cars, or anything! To the pilot, the island was totally deserted—the way it had been before the airfield had been built! Eventually, the pilot just flew away, still thinking she was lost.

You can't even trust your eyes in the Bermuda Triangle! Perhaps the most famous case was the flight of five torpedo bombers which took off from Fort Lauderdale in Florida on December 5, 1945. It was just an ordinary training flight—but the planes never returned. Somehow, these very experienced pilots got lost. Their compasses and then their radios stopped working properly—and they kept heading away from safety. The last message from the flight leader said that things looked "wrong" and "strange" to them. No one will ever know what he meant, because the flight just disappeared. And so did a huge aircraft sent up to search for them!

There are many, many cases of missing ships in the Triangle, but the most famous is the Marie Celeste. The Marie Celeste was found in 1872, floating abandoned in the Triangle, with all sails set. But there was not a single person on board! Even though there was food and water, and the ship was in good condition, the crew was gone. They had disappeared without taking even their pipes or tobacco. What happened? Was it aliens? A waterspout? People from Atlantis? Did a monster octopus drag them to their deaths? No one will ever be able to say for sure—but some weird things are happening in the Bermuda Triangle!

Comprehend It!

A STRANGE TRIANGLE

Level A

1. Why do people think the Bermuda Triangle is special?

   _____

   _____

2. Name two of the weird things that might happen in the Triangle.

   _____   _____

3. Which is the most famous of the missing ships in the Triangle?

   _____

4. In the story about the pilot who became lost, was the pilot male or female?

   _____

Level B

1. What might happen to a sailing boat if the compass didn't work properly?

   _____

   _____

2. Why do you think the Bermuda Triangle has received more publicity in the last twenty years or so? _____

   _____

   _____

3. Why didn't the Fort Lauderdale torpedo bombers just turn around and head back to safety? _____

   _____

   _____

4. What tells you the *Marie Celeste*'s crew left in a hurry?

   _____

   _____

   _____

Comprehend It!

A STRANGE TRIANGLE

Level C

1. Do you think the writer believes there is something funny about the Bermuda Triangle? Why? _____

    _____

    _____

2. What *facts* does the writer present to support the claims in the article?

    _____

    _____

3. What do you think is the most likely reason the crew disappeared from the *Marie Celeste*? What do you think is the *least* likely reason?

    _____

    _____

    _____

    _____

4. You are the flight leader in the flight of aircraft from Fort Lauderdale. In a paragraph or two, describe what you are seeing that is "wrong" and "strange."

    _____

    _____

    _____

    _____

    _____

    _____

    _____

    _____

    _____

ATLANTIS—LOST OR FOUND?

Somewhere in the world is said to be the remains of the fabulous lost continent of Atlantis. According to legend, Atlantis existed about 50,000 years ago, in the *Atlantic* Ocean, somewhere beyond the Pillars of Hercules. The people of Atlantis, the Atlanteans, were supposed to be very advanced in science and engineering—even more advanced than we are today. They were said to have found the secret of unlimited energy and power, using crystals to harness their energy.

Gradually, the stories about Atlanteans grew and grew: they could fly in anti-gravity machines or spaceships; they had weapons like lasers, and talking computers; they could communicate telepathically. When Hollywood got hold of the legend, some movies even had the Atlanteans still alive today, living in huge domed cities beneath the sea!

Then, so the original legend goes, something happened, and Atlantis was destroyed, along with all its people. Just what happened, we are not sure. One story is that it was a natural disaster, like an earthquake or volcano, or both together, that sank Atlantis without a trace. Another story says that the Atlanteans discovered powers they couldn't control, which eventually broke loose and destroyed them.

At the start of this century, scientists discovered, buried under the earth of Greece, the remains of an entire civilization, unlike anything they had seen before. They began to think they may have discovered Atlantis. To add to their beliefs, the neighboring island of Thera seemed to have been responsible for a giant volcanic eruption that destroyed Atlantis.

Despite this proof, many people still did not believe Atlantis had been found. Thanks to films, television and writers with terrific imaginations, the favorite spot for finding Atlantis was not Greece but—the Bermuda Triangle. And in 1968, that looked to be coming true, when divers discovered steps, pathways, walls and even pyramids under the water off the coast of Bimini, in the Bermuda Triangle. There was huge excitement! It looked as if Atlantis had finally been discovered. What's more, if Atlantis *was* beneath the Bermuda Triangle, it could help to explain some of the strange things that happened there! Perhaps some of those Atlantean machines, with powers we can't even understand, were still working under the ocean.

But, as usually happens, the next lot of divers to investigate the area said the whole thing was a load of rubbish! All they could find were natural rock formations that looked a *little* bit like walls and roads, but certainly no cities, or pyramids, or strange machines.

But people still keep looking. Perhaps they are wasting their time, perhaps Atlantis never existed at all. Or maybe they just haven't looked in the right places—like under the snow and ice at the Poles. Maybe it's just that people *need* stories like Atlantis to give them something to imagine—and dream about.

ATLANTIS—LOST OR FOUND?

Level A

1. What were the people of Atlantis called?

2. According to the original legend, in which ocean was Atlantis to be found?

3. Why did scientists believe they had discovered Atlantis in Greece?

4. Where is the favorite spot for finding Atlantis?

Level B

1. What does the writer mean by saying, "When Hollywood got hold of the legend …"?

2. Why do you think people believed that divers had found the ruins of cities beneath the ocean off Bermuda?

3. What happened after the discovery was announced?

4. If Atlantis was discovered in the Bermuda Triangle, how would that explain some of the weird things that happen there?

Comprehend It!

ATLANTIS—LOST OR FOUND?

Level C

1. Do you think scientists have taken the idea of Atlantis seriously? Explain your answer.

2. Do you think that the writer believes in the existence of Atlantis? Why?

3. In your own words, explain why you think people are still searching for Atlantis.

4. You are a diver who has just found ruins on the ocean floor in the Bermuda Triangle. In a paragraph or two, describe what you are seeing.

CYCLE

He dreamed someone was shaking his shoulder.

"Mike! *Mike!* Wake up, Mike!"

Someone *was* shaking his shoulder. Mike opened his eyes slowly; his eyelids felt as if they had been glued together. It was his mother. "Come on, you couch potato! Get in the car. You can come shopping with me instead of lying on that couch sleeping in front of the television."

"But, Mom...."

"Don't 'But, Mom' me, Mike. You are not, repeat *not*, spending your school vacation lying around the house. You'll go back to school looking like a beach ball!" Mom bent and picked up two empty potato chip packets and a cool drink can from the floor. "The rules are no more than one hour's TV during the day—and *no* snacking between meals unless I say so. Have you got that?"

"That's not fair," Mike mumbled.

"I beg your pardon?"

"Nothing, Mom." He sighs.

In the car on the way to the store, Mike stared gloomily out of the window. It just wasn't fair. There were nearly two weeks of the vacation left, and Mom was going to make him exercise and eat healthy foods. And how could he watch a video if he was only allowed one hour of TV a day? It was worse than being in prison. Maybe he should run away. Yeah, that'd be cool. Then they'd all be worried about him and go on TV and say things like, "We love you, Mikey. Please come home. You can watch TV twenty-four-hours-a-day if you want. We'll buy you your own TV and video recorder and CD player. And we'll serve you hot dogs, and nachos, and chicken nuggets with chips every hour, and...."

Something made Mike look up just before the truck backed out into the road ahead of them. "Look out!" he screamed and his Mom swung the steering wheel and slammed on the brakes. But it was too late. The truck clipped the side of their car and then they were rolling—over and over and over and over—and Mike could see the world turning like a merry-go-round gone crazy. Then it all went black.

He dreamed someone was shaking his shoulder.

"Mike! *Mike!* Wake up, Mike!"

Someone *was* shaking his shoulder. Mike opened his eyes slowly; his eyelids felt as if they had been glued together. It was his mother. "Come on, you couch potato! Get in the car. You can come shopping with me instead of lying on that couch sleeping in front of the television."

Comprehend It!

CYCLE

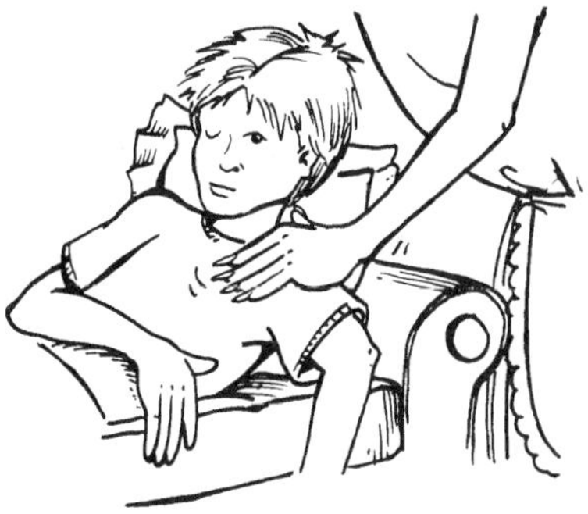

Level A

1. Name three foods that Mike liked to eat.

   _____

   _____

   _____

2. Why did his mother call him a couch potato? _____

   _____

3. How much of the school vacation was left? _____

   _____

4. What had Mike eaten while he was watching television?

   _____

   _____

Level B

1. Explain the title of the story.

   _____

   _____

2. What should be the next line in the story?

   _____

3. What does the writer mean by, "Then it all went black"?

   _____

   _____

4. Use your own words to describe what a "merry-go-round gone crazy" means.

   _____

   _____

   _____

Comprehend It!

CYCLE

Level C

1. Would it be fair to call Mike a lazy person? Explain your answer.

2. Why did Mike say being at home was "... worse than being in prison"?

3. While he is in the car, Mike has a daydream. Is it the type of daydream he *would* have? Explain your answer.

4. Do you think it *was* all a dream? In your own words, in a paragraph or two, write what happens next.

Comprehend It!

BATTERIES INCLUDED

There was *definitely* something strange about Melissa's new teacher, Miss Matthews. But when Melissa spoke to her friends about it, they thought she was imagining things.

"Don't be silly," said her best friend in the world, Samantha. "She's just the same as any other person."

"Weird?" said Kylie. "Lissie, *all* teachers are weird; this one's no different!"

"Nonsense, dear," said her Mom, when Melissa told her. "I'm sure you're just imagining it. Once you get used to Miss Matthews, you'll find she is just like everyone else."

"She'd have to be weird to teach you, anyway," said Melissa's younger sister, Jessica.

"Not half as weird as after teaching *you* for a week," Melissa replied sweetly.

"That's enough out of you two," said their Dad from behind his newspaper. He'd heard it all before. "Set the table and stop arguing."

But later that night in bed, just before she fell asleep, Melissa decided that she was right after all —there *was* something weird about Miss Matthews. And she was going to find out what it was!

The following day, she put her plan into action. It wasn't much of a plan, really. All she could think of was to follow Miss Matthews for the whole day at school, and try not to let her out of her sight.

At morning recess, Miss Matthews went into the teachers' room and just sat at one of the tables. She didn't have a cup of coffee or a cookie. None of the other teachers spoke to her, either, which Melissa thought was rude.

Miss Matthews did the same thing at lunch time, until Mrs. Hoi-Poi, the principal, whispered something in her ear. Then Miss Matthews stood up and went out and did playground duty.

But at afternoon recess, Miss Matthews did something different. Instead of going into the teachers' room, she went into the office. She knocked on Mrs. Hoi-Poi's door and stood and waited until it was opened. She went inside the room and the door closed behind her.

Melissa raced around the office block and scooted up the branches of a small tree. From there she could see straight into the office windows, without being seen herself. It was against school rules to climb the trees, but just then Melissa couldn't have cared less. When she saw what was happening, she nearly fell out of the tree with surprise anyway!

Mrs. Hoi-Poi had a long electrical cord in one hand. One end was plugged into a wall socket. With her free hand, she reached out and swept up Miss Matthews' hair. Miss Matthews just stood there, not moving.

Then Mrs. Hoi-Poi plugged the power cord into the socket in the back of Miss Matthews' neck.

BATTERIES INCLUDED

Level A

1. What was Melissa's nickname? How do you know?

   _____

   _____

2. How many children were there in Melissa's family?

   _____

3. What job did Mrs. Hoi-Poi have in the school?

   _____

4. What was the first weird thing Melissa noticed when she started watching Miss Matthews? _____

   _____

Level B

1. What do you think Miss Matthews was? What tells you this?

   _____

   _____

2. Do you think Melissa and Jessica tease each other often? What tells you this?

   _____

   _____

3. Were the other teachers being rude when they didn't talk to Miss Matthews in the teachers' room? Why?

   _____

   _____

   _____

4. Why do you think Miss Matthews didn't eat or drink anything in the teachers' room?

   _____

   _____

BATTERIES INCLUDED

Level C

1. What would be the advantages of having Miss Matthews for a teacher? What would be the disadvantages? _____
   _____
   _____

2. What do you think Mrs. Hoi-Poi whispered in Miss Matthews' ear?
   _____
   _____

3. Discuss the title of the story. Create another title of your own.
   _____
   _____

4. In a paragraph, describe to the rest of the class what Melissa has just seen.
   _____
   _____
   _____
   _____
   _____
   _____
   _____
   _____
   _____
   _____
   _____
   _____

"I WANT TO DRINK YOUR BLOOD..."

It is 1732 in Yugoslavia. You are a soldier, one of twenty-four sent from Belgrade with other government officials and officers to investigate a report of a vampire in a small country town. The sun is just beginning to set as you march to the grave where the suspected vampire lies. The headstone shows that the person in the grave, a man, died three years ago. Yet, in the past few weeks, he is supposed to have killed five of his nieces and nephews, sucking them dry of their blood. You begin to dig.

Finally, the coffin is opened. Inside is the man. You cannot believe your eyes. He looks to be perfectly healthy, as if he is just asleep. An officer bravely places his hand on the "vampire's" chest—and cries out when he detects a heartbeat!

Immediately, he orders a steel bar to be hammered through the vampire's chest and into his heart. As the bar pierces the heart, fresh red blood, mixed with a white fluid, spurts out. The body is buried again, in lime this time, and there are no more reports of vampires from that village.

Sound like a good fairy story? A script for a movie? Well, it's neither of those. It's actually recorded in history as a *true story*. But does that mean vampires are true; that they actually exist?

No, not really. But during that time in Europe, people believed absolutely and utterly that there were such things as vampires. And if you believe in something that strongly, your mind can twist things to make them appear to be the way you expect them to be. Where did the stories about vampires come from then? No one knows for sure, but there are a few ideas about it.

Back then, it wasn't unusual for people to be buried in special tombs called mausoleums. Often, they were buried with treasures and offerings of food and wine. Starving beggars would break into these mausoleums at night to steal what they could and, because it was usually dry inside, to sleep out of the rain. If anyone saw one of these people in the moonlight—or even worse, saw one "wake up" from the dead—you can imagine their fear, and the story they would later tell!

Another reason for a belief in vampires could be plain, simple ignorance. "Doctors" during these times knew nothing about trances or comas; even as late as the mid-1800s there was still confusion among doctors as to how you could tell when someone was really dead. Up until recent times, it is probably true to say that literally thousands and thousands of people were buried alive. Imagine coming out of a coma to find yourself being buried in a coffin. Or, just as bad, imagine yourself in the position of an undertaker, when the corpse suddenly sits up and comes back to life.

Very few people today still believe in vampires; such creatures just have no foundation in truth. But there is one funny thing, though. Have you ever noticed how, after your teacher has been giving you a hard time and making you work like a slave all day, you feel very tired—sort of ... *drained?* Makes you stop and think about teachers, doesn't it!

Comprehend It!

"I WANT TO DRINK YOUR BLOOD ..."

Level A

1. How long had the dead man been in the coffin?

2. Why did the officer cry out?

3. Does this article tell you that vampires were real? Explain your answer.

4. Give two reasons why the stories about vampires might have started.

Level B

1. In your own words, what is this article trying to tell you?

2. Why do you think people would be buried with treasures, food and wine?

3. How do you kill a vampire?

4. Why were people in earlier times more likely to believe in vampires than we are today?

Comprehend It!

"I WANT TO DRINK YOUR BLOOD ..."

Level C

1. Which do you think would be worse: waking up to find yourself buried alive; or being an undertaker and suddenly having one of the corpses sit up? Why?

   _____
   _____
   _____
   _____

2. Why do you think the writer places the word "Doctors" in quotation marks when speaking about the 1700s? _____

   _____
   _____

3. How well does the writer explain what vampires really were? Why?

   _____
   _____

4. Using your imagination, write an explanation for what *werewolves* might have really been.

   _____
   _____
   _____
   _____
   _____
   _____
   _____
   _____

Comprehend It!

THEY JUST DISAPPEARED

What happened to the dinosaurs? About sixty-five million years ago, these creatures, which had ruled the earth for many millions of years, suddenly died out. Why? How?

One explanation is that it simply grew too cold for them. Apparently, about that time there *was* a general cooling down of the earth and the dinosaurs died. And how did that happen?

The most popular theory is that the earth was hit by a *very* large meteorite. The impact created an explosion which threw a huge cloud of debris and dirt into the upper atmosphere, where it drifted around for a long time. This cloud was so thick, it partially blocked the sun's rays—and so the earth cooled down a little. Unable to adapt to such a rapid temperature change, the dinosaurs died out. This theory is given support by the fact that many other creatures—both on land and in the sea—died out at about the same time, which is what *would* happen in the event of such a large catastrophe.

One immediate argument against this theory is that no crater large enough has ever been found. But what if the meteorite landed in the sea, or on a part of the earth that is now under the sea? There are many areas beneath the sea that have not yet been explored, and probably won't be in our lifetime.

Thanks to television, movies and books, you'll hear many other stories about what caused the dinosaurs to become extinct. But, not so strangely, you won't find many facts presented to back these theories up.

One popular story is that the dinosaurs were destroyed by aliens who wanted to populate the planet with their own creatures—humans. According to this theory, the dinosaurs were too much of a threat, and so they were wiped out. If *any* evidence is found to support this theory, it will cause an absolute sensation. But so far, as you might guess, nothing has been found.

Another theory is that the earth's vegetation changed quickly, and the dinosaurs were poisoned when they ate this vegetation, or when they killed and ate prey that had been feeding on the vegetation. Unfortunately for the people who believe in this theory, scientists now know that new species of dinosaurs were evolving all the time, right up until they died out—including many herbivores that were able to eat and thrive on the new vegetation.

What it all boils down to is that, like most mysteries, no one really knows the answer for sure. You might even be wondering what all the fuss is about when it happened so many millions of years ago. Well, think about this. The dinosaurs ruled the earth for many millions of years, and yet they died out almost overnight in geological terms. Humans have only been around for a bit less than four million years. How long will we last?

Comprehend It!

THEY JUST DISAPPEARED

Level A

1. Approximately how long has it been since dinosaurs have been on the earth?
   _____

2. True or false: Dinosaurs were a threat to early humans. (Explain your answer.)
   _____
   _____

3. Give the most likely reason why the dinosaurs died out.
   _____
   _____

4. If a giant meteorite did hit the earth in the past, why haven't we found the crater? _____
   _____

Level B

1. Does the writer believe that aliens wiped out the dinosaurs?
   Explain your answer. _____
   _____

2. Why would any evidence that aliens destroyed the dinosaurs and put humans on the earth cause "an absolute sensation"?
   _____
   _____

3. Which is the most likely theory to explain how the dinosaurs died out?
   _____
   _____

4. Why does it make any difference how the dinosaurs died out?
   _____
   _____

Comprehend It!

THEY JUST DISAPPEARED

Level C

1. Why do you think there are so many theories about what happened to the dinosaurs?

   _____

   _____

2. You have just gone back in time and come face to face with a dinosaur. Describe how you feel.

   _____

   _____

3. Considering humans weren't even around then, why do think people today are so fascinated by dinosaurs?

   _____

   _____

4. In your own words, in a paragraph or two, describe another theory explaining how the dinosaurs died out.

   _____

   _____

   _____

   _____

   _____

   _____

   _____

   _____

   _____

   _____

   _____

   _____

   _____

PREMONITION

Julia was frightened—and tired. She'd had the same dream every night now for a week. Each night, it had woken her up, crying. And each time she had been too afraid to go back to sleep, so she had just lain in bed until the sun rose and the world came back to life. She hadn't told her parents about the dream. They would be worried about her, and she didn't want to spoil their vacation; she knew how much they were looking forward to it. She was lucky they had been letting her sleep in her own motel room, or they surely would have heard her crying in the night.

It wasn't even as if she could make any sense of the dream. In it, a giant arrowhead came plunging from the sky. Revolving gracefully, falling in slow motion, it headed straight for her. Julia couldn't tell what it was—but she knew if it hit her she was dead. In this dream, she was sitting down. She felt she should get up and run, but something was stopping her. In desperation, Julia looked at her waist. A thick rope was tied around it, knotted in front, holding her in place. Desperately, she tore at the rope until her fingernails bent back and broke.

But she couldn't get the knot undone.

The arrowhead loomed larger and larger, filling her vision, blocking out the sun, until …

She would wake up crying.

"Are you OK, dear?" her mother asked from the front seat of the car. "I've been speaking to you for the last minute or two, and I'm sure you haven't heard a word I've said."

"Sorry, Mom. I was a million miles away. What did you say?"

"I was just telling you that we're almost at Potter's Peak. We'll stay the night in the new motel there. It's called "The Pyramid." According to the guide book, it has a lot of facilities for guests, including tennis courts, in-house movies, a sauna and a spa."

"Sounds great, Mom." All Julia really wanted to do was to lie down and try to get some sleep.

The motel *was* very modern. Dad eased the car to a stop in front of the office. Above them, a model of an Egyptian pyramid with the motel's name on it rotated slowly on a metal pole. Something about it stabbed Julia's heart with an icy knife. She reached for her seatbelt, but the buckle jammed and she couldn't unbuckle it.

"Dad! Dad!" she screamed, suddenly understanding. "Shift the car! Quickly! Shift the car!"

Her father, startled, jerked the accelerator and the car, still in gear, shot forward, before he got it under control. He turned in his seat, his face red from fright at her shouting.

And the pyramid sign, slowly and still revolving gracefully, fell from the roof of the motel to crash to earth where they had been just seconds before.

Comprehend It!

PREMONITION

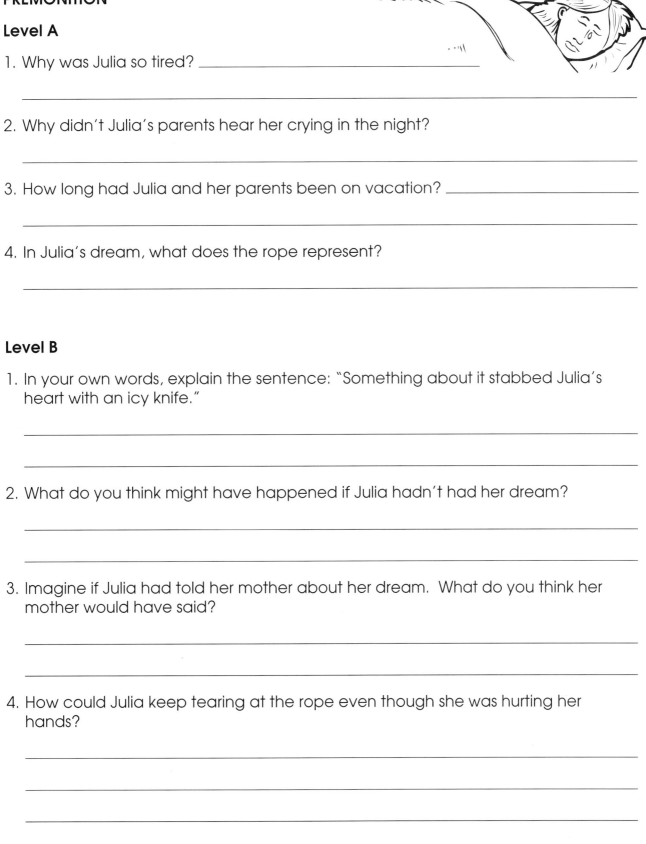

Level A

1. Why was Julia so tired? _____

2. Why didn't Julia's parents hear her crying in the night?

3. How long had Julia and her parents been on vacation? _____

4. In Julia's dream, what does the rope represent?

Level B

1. In your own words, explain the sentence: "Something about it stabbed Julia's heart with an icy knife."

2. What do you think might have happened if Julia hadn't had her dream?

3. Imagine if Julia had told her mother about her dream. What do you think her mother would have said?

4. How could Julia keep tearing at the rope even though she was hurting her hands?

Comprehend It!

PREMONITION

Level C

1. How appropriate is the title of the story? Why? What else could it be called?

2. How old do you think Julia is? What makes you think this?

3. The writer doesn't explain the meaning of Julia's dream, but leaves it to you to figure it out. How successful is this? Explain.

4. Imagine you are Julia. A television news team is reporting the event. How will you explain your dream to them? Write down the questions they might ask and the answers you would give.

A HELPING HAND

Kelvin was lost. There was no other way to describe it, he was lost! And after his father had told him not to wander away from the picnic grounds too. He was so sure he could find his way back, but he'd been walking now for an hour and a half—and he didn't have the foggiest idea where he was. He sat on a fallen tree and put his chin in his hands.

"Help! Help! H E L P!!!" he screamed, wishing there was someone to hear him.

"Is there a problem?" asked a quiet voice beside him, startling Kelvin into falling from the tree. "I don't like to hear young people get upset, whatever the reason. You *do* have a reason, don't you?"

The speaker was an old man dressed in dark, uncomfortable-looking clothes and heavy black boots. He had a thick beard, shot full of gray; eyebrows that squatted over his eyes like verandas, and a battered and shapeless hat pushed to the back of his head. Whoever he was, Kelvin was glad to see him.

"S-s-s-sorry I s-s-screamed," he stuttered. "B-b-but I'm lost."

"Lost! Lost? What nonsense," the man said. "You know where you are—it's just the other people who don't know where you are. Right?" Kelvin nodded. "Of course I'm right," the man went on. He stopped and looked up suddenly, as if he'd heard a noise. "Hmm," he said. "They're lookin' for you, you know—in the wrong places. City people!" He almost spat the last words out. "Come on, young 'un, follow me."

They walked for kilometers, the man pointing out all sorts of interesting things along the way, like animal tracks and tiny, hidden flowers. Finally, they came to a large, flat area that stretched away to the left and right as far as Kelvin could see. On the other side, however, he could just make out people and cars—the search party, he hoped!

"Better take those fancy running shoes off," said the old man.

"Why?"

"'Cause that's mud, sonny, 'n' if you don't take 'em off, it'll suck 'em off your feet. OK?"

Kelvin did as he was told, then stepped into the thick, clingy mud that came past his ankles. With his new friend walking beside him, he started across.

His father was startled to see Kelvin slip and slop his way out of the mud.

"How did you find us?" he asked in amazement.

"My f-f-f-friend showed me the way," Kelvin explained.

"What friend?" Dad asked, still puzzled.

Kelvin turned to show him, and saw just a single set of footprints leading across the mud—his own.

Comprehend It!

A HELPING HAND

Level A

1. Was Kelvin from the city or the country?

   How do you know? _____
   _____

2. True or false?:
   Kelvin was wearing fancy black riding boots.
   _____

3. Why did Kelvin scream?
   _____
   _____

4. Why was Kelvin's father startled to see him? _____
   _____

Level B

1. In your own words, explain why Kelvin wasn't lost, according to the old man.
   _____
   _____

2. Why do you think Kelvin wished there was someone to hear him scream?
   _____
   _____

3. Do you think Kelvin would be in trouble for getting lost? Explain your answer.
   _____
   _____

4. How could Kelvin explain his experience with the man to his father?
   _____
   _____
   _____

A HELPING HAND

Level C

1. Who—or what—do *you* think the old man was?

   _____

   _____

2. Why did the old man disappear when Kelvin was safe? _____

   _____

3. Explain why the writer describes the old man's eyebrows by saying they "squatted over his eyes like verandas."

   _____

   _____

4. Rewrite the ending of the story so the old man *doesn't* disappear at the last minute. Have him explain to Kelvin's father who he is.

   _____

   _____

   _____

   _____

   _____

   _____

   _____

   _____

   _____

   _____

   _____

   _____

 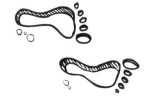 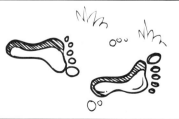

ARE WE THE FIRST?

If we accept scientific theory, the earth is many, many millions of years old. Yet humans have only been on it for a very short time. Or have they? People who believe that this is not the first time the earth has been populated by humans, like to point out the following strange facts. Those who don't believe this theory simply say that these facts are untrue, or can be easily explained as normal.

1. A footprint was found in limestone in Pershing County, Nevada. It shows the sole of a shoe, and is so clear you can see the rows of double stitching. Yet the rock the footprint is in is dated at 400 million years old!

2. A strange bell-shaped container, shaped a bit like a school bell, and patterned with flowers made from pure silver, was dynamited out of solid rock four meters below the ground in Massachusetts in 1851. It was reported in the *Scientific American* magazine.

3. In 1928 in Oklahoma, a miner in a coal mine, after firing explosives to break up the coal, discovered a wall made of polished concrete blocks about thirty centimeters square. This was approximately 3,000 meters underground.

4. Manuscripts many thousands of years old, translated in Mysore, India, in 1952, included a design for the construction of a vertical-flight transport aircraft (like a helicopter with wings) for carrying ammunition, as well as the plans for passenger planes that could carry up to 500 people.

5. Two skulls, 3,500 years old, found in Armenia, Europe in 1972, showed that the women, when alive, had undergone brain surgery of the most delicate kind, involving boring into the skull and then plugging the wound with shaped animal bone—and had lived for up to fifteen years after the successful operation.

6. Ruins of ancient buildings in Scotland, Turkey and Arabia have been discovered where so much heat has been applied to them some time in the past that bricks and skeletons have turned to carbon, sand has turned to glass, and even the rocks have melted and flowed like water. Today, such heat is only known in a nuclear explosion.

7. An African tribe, the Dogon, as part of their folklore which has been handed down from generation to generation for thousands of years, tell how Sirius is actually a double star, that its invisible other half is the heaviest of all stars and that it revolves around Sirius once every fifty years. It wasn't until 1862 that modern scientists discovered that Sirius *does* have another partner, which *does* revolve once every fifty years around Sirius and that, because it is a white dwarf star, this partner is *extremely* heavy for its relatively small size! But how did a primitive African tribe know this?

There are many cases such as these. In fact, whole books have been written about them and movies made about them. Much of what is claimed can be easily disproved as simply wild imagination. But there are some things that, while they may not prove anything, are just too weird and mysterious to be easily explained.

ARE WE THE FIRST?

Level A

1. How far underground was the wall of concrete blocks?

2. Which African tribe knows all about Sirius?

3. The stories in the article are all true. True or false?

4. What do you need to turn sand to glass?

Level B

1. In one sentence, write in your own words the main idea of the article.

2. What's so strange about finding the plans for aircraft in India?

3. Why do you think it is important for the writer to mention that the bell-shaped container was reported in the *Scientific American* magazine?

4. Give a normal explanation for the footprints in the limestone.

Comprehend It!

ARE WE THE FIRST?

Level C

1. Look at any three of the seven strange facts. How would you prove or disprove them?

   _____
   _____
   _____

2. What do you think—are we the first? Why? _____
   _____
   _____
   _____

3. In a paragraph or two, tell the story of finding the underground concrete blocks from the miner's point of view.

   _____
   _____
   _____
   _____
   _____
   _____
   _____
   _____
   _____
   _____

TUNGUSKA

Just after 7:00 a.m. on June 30, 1908, an enormous explosion occurred over an extremely remote area near the Stony Tunguska River in what was then called Russia. Although it was nearly twenty years later before the actual site was examined, there were many eyewitnesses to the explosion. Their reports were startling.

They told how a cigar-shaped object, as bright as the sun and trailing smoke, raced across the sky with a deafening roar, before exploding into a pillar of fire and a mushroom-shaped cloud of black smoke that reached some twenty kilometers high. Scientists later calculated the force of that explosion as equal to somewhere around thirty-five million tons of TNT. This makes it as large as the largest hydrogen bomb explosion.

The blast was so large that the shock waves from it traveled twice around the earth through the atmosphere before fading away. Seismic waves (earthquake waves) were detected as far away as Washington, DC. It also caused the sky to glow strangely at night. People in London actually panicked because the nights were so bright. While closer to the blast it was possible to take photographs at midnight—without a flash!

In 1927, a Russian professor finally reached Tunguska with a team of scientists. He found an area of devastation of almost 2,000 square kilometers, where trees and all vegetation had been flattened and incinerated black. Their roots all pointed to the center of the blast. The professor investigated further, expecting to find a huge meteorite crater. To his surprise, there was no crater, just a number of small holes a few meters across. What on earth had caused the explosion then, if not a meteorite?

It wasn't until much later, after World War II, that scientists recognized the effects as being the same as those to be found after an aerial nuclear explosion. But Tunguska happened more than thirty years *before* the first atomic bombs were invented.

Then came the most controversial explanation of all—that the strange object had been a damaged alien spacecraft and the explosion had been caused when its nuclear-powered engine detonated. At first, this explanation was dismissed by everyone. But when the statements by the eyewitnesses were examined, researchers were surprised to find that the object had made several sharp course changes before exploding—*as though it was being controlled.* This was something a meteorite did *not* do.

Today, however, it is generally accepted that the Tunguska explosion *was* caused by a special type of meteorite—but this still can not be proved. Until it *is* proved, it must remain a possibility that it just *could* have been some sort of alien spacecraft. What do you think?

TUNGUSKA

Level A

1. Why was it possible to take photographs at midnight near Tunguska in 1908?

2. Why didn't scientists at first recognize the blast effects were the same as those of an aerial nuclear explosion?

3. Apart from a meteorite, what did some people think caused the explosion?

4. True or false:

    Meteorites often make sharp turns in the atmosphere before exploding.

Level B

1. Why did the roots of the trees all point to the center of the blast?

2. If all this took place in an extremely remote area of Russia, how is it that the exact date and time of the explosion are known?

3. Why is it possible that the eyewitnesses' stories may not have been 100% reliable?

4. If it was suddenly proved that the explosion was an alien spaceship, what effect would it have on science and scientists?

Comprehend It!

TUNGUSKA

Level C

1. What do you feel the writer believes happened at Tunguska? Why?

   _____
   _____
   _____

2. Why were the eyewitness reports "startling"?

   _____
   _____

3. Many people would *like* to believe the Tunguska explosion was caused by a spaceship. Why do you think this might be?

   _____
   _____

4. You are an eyewitness to the Tunguska explosion. Write down your story for a newspaper report.

   _____
   _____
   _____
   _____
   _____
   _____
   _____
   _____
   _____
   _____
   _____
   _____
   _____

ASKING DIRECTIONS

When Li had decided to cycle home from her best friend Maria's house, she hadn't been nervous. After all, she had lived in the country all her life, she was twelve years old and certainly not afraid of the dark, and it was only a twenty-minute ride home anyway. But halfway home, when she couldn't see the lights of either farmhouse, she began to wish she hadn't been quite so brave, and had accepted a ride home from Mr. Zampatti. She pedalled faster.

She went round a slight bend in the gravel road, where the woods were thick and the trees seemed to reach for her in the pale moonlight—and it suddenly got cold—very cold! There was a thick white fog, hanging in layers above the road, and misting the top branches of the trees. Li's breath puffed in thick clouds in front of her, and her bare legs were so cold they felt like they were burning.

Her heart was thumping loudly and she was panting as she pedalled away at top speed, so that she didn't hear the car until it suddenly appeared beside her like a silent black ghost. She squealed to herself and skidded to a stop. The big black limousine also stopped, the brake lights glowing bright red in the mist. The gravel scrunched as it reversed down the road to Li. She thought it was the quietest car she had ever heard—or not heard.

The car stopped alongside her. She tried to look inside, but the windows were tinted almost black and she could see nothing. Then the window on the passenger's side began to slide silently down—and Li found she was holding her breath, too frightened even to move!

In the soft glow of the many instruments, Li saw something move inside. Then a very bright light suddenly clicked on, and Li found herself staring at—a little gray-haired old lady! The relief was so great, Li almost burst into giggles—or tears. But she managed to control herself.

"Hello, dear," said the little old lady. "Can you help me? I'm afraid I'm lost. Can you tell me where I might find the nearest airport? It's very important. I have to be there in the next five minutes."

"Airport? I'll say you're lost," Li said, getting off her bike and walking closer to the car. She could feel a strange tingle coming from it, like static electricity. "You have to go back down this road the way you've just come for about ten kilometers. Then, when the road forks, take the left fork for another ten or so kilometers. That puts you back on the main highway. Then you turn right and follow the signs for about another twenty kilometers. I'm afraid there's no way you're going to make it in the next five minutes though."

"Thank you very much, dear; you're very kind to an old lady. And don't worry; I'll make it in plenty of time."

The window wound up again and the car moved off. A little way ahead, it did a three-point turn and came back. The headlights flashed as it went past Li, and she smiled and waved. Poor old dear, she thought. She hasn't got a chance. She turned to give a final wave—and froze.

The car was changing. First the color was fading—from black to a silvery-gray. While that was happening, the wheels were disappearing into the arches, though the car kept going forward, floating above the ground. Then the big, round red tail-lights began to grow, until they were the size of rubbish bin lids, glowing more and more brightly all the while.

Then the car lifted into the dark sky and, with a faint whistling sound, was gone faster than the eye could follow.

ASKING DIRECTIONS

Level A

1. What was Maria's last name?

2. How far was the car from the airport?

3. What made Li hold her breath, "too frightened even to move"?

4. Why did Li feel like laughing—or crying?

Level B

1. Is it important that it suddenly got very cold? Why?

2. Why does the writer describe the car as a "silent black ghost"?

3. What clues does the writer give you during the story that the car is not all it seems to be?

4. What do you think Li did after the car took off?

Comprehend It!

ASKING DIRECTIONS

Level C

1. At what point in the story does it move from reality to fantasy?

   _____

2. "Asking Directions" is a very down-to-earth title. For what reasons do you think the writer chose this title? What else might it have been called?

   _____
   _____
   _____

3. Why would the writer make the driver of the car a "little gray-haired old lady"?

   _____
   _____
   _____

4. Put yourself in Li's shoes. In a paragraph or two, explain to your parents what has just happened to you in a way that will make them believe your story!

   _____
   _____
   _____
   _____
   _____
   _____
   _____
   _____
   _____
   _____

Comprehend It!

ANSWERS

SPECIAL NOTE:
Only Level A questions are literal; the remainder all require a certain amount of interpretation. Therefore, only Level A questions can have right or wrong answers.

The validity of answers to questions in Levels B and C will be left to individual teachers and/or students to determine.

A STRANGE TRIANGLE – page 7
Level A
1. Because of the reported strange happenings there
2. Compass deflection/time and/or visual distortion
3. *Marie Celeste*
4. Female (*... still thinking she was lost.*)

ATLANTIS–LOST OR FOUND? – page 10
Level A
1. Atlanteans
2. Atlantic
3. They found a buried civilization unlike any other
4. The Bermuda Triangle

CYCLE – page 13
Level A
1. Potato chips/hot dogs/nachos/chicken nuggets/chips
2. He was lying on the couch watching TV/eating
3. Nearly two weeks
4. Two packets of potato chips and a cool drink

BATTERIES INCLUDED – page 16
Level A
1. Lissie. Kylie calls her that.
2. Two
3. Principal
4. No coffee in the teacher's lounge/just sat there/did not speak/no one spoke to her

"I WANT TO DRINK YOUR BLOOD..." – page 19
Level A
1. Three years
2. The "body" had a heartbeat
3. No. It gives reasons against the belief in their reality.
4. Mistaken identity/Ignorance (mistakenly declared dead)

THEY JUST DISAPPEARED – page 22
Level A
1. About sixty-five million years
2. False. No humans lived on earth then.
3. Meteorite strike/cooling down of earth
4. It could be underwater

PREMONITION – page 25
Level A
1. Her dream woke her up every night
2. She had a separate room
3. A week
4. The car seatbelt (Something holding her back)

A HELPING HAND – page 28
Level A
1. The city. The old man says "City people!".
2. False (Fancy running shoes)
3. He was lost/he would be in trouble
4. He was supposed to be lost

ARE WE THE FIRST? – page 31
Level A
1. Approximately 3,000 meters
2. The Dogon
3. False (No proof is given)
4. Extreme heat

TUNGUSKA – page 34
Level A
1. Because of the glow in the sky
2. Because in 1908 they didn't have nuclear explosions
3. An exploding spaceship
4. False

ASKING DIRECTIONS – page 37
Level A
1. Zampatti
2. About forty kilometers
3. The car and the window sliding down
4. Relief (at seeing just a little gray-haired lady in the car)

Books Available from World Teachers Press®

MATH

A Blast of Math
  Grades 3-4, 4-5, 5-6, 6-7
Math Word Puzzles
  Grades 5-8
Mastergrids for Math
  Elementary Resource
Essential Facts and Tables
  Grades 3-10
Math Puzzles Galore
  Grades 4-8
Practice Math
  Grades 4, 5, 6, 7
Math Speed Tests
  Grades 1-3, 3-6
Problem Solving with Math
  Grades 2-3, 4-5, 6-8
Math Through Language
  Grades 1-2, 2-3, 3-4
Exploring Measurement
  Grades 2-3, 3-4, 5-6
Chance, Statistics & Graphs
  Grades 1-3, 3-5
Step Into Tables
  Elementary
Problem Solving Through Investigation
  Grades 5-8, 7-10
The Early Fraction Book
  Grades 3-4
The Fraction Book
  Grades 5-8
It's About Time
  Grades 2-3, 4-5
Do It Write Math
  Grades 2-3
Mental Math Workouts
  Grades 4-6, 5-7, 6-8, 7-9
Math Grid Games
  Grades 4-8
High Interest Mathematics
  Grades 5-8
Math Homework Assignments
  Grades 2, 3, 4, 5, 6, 7
Visual Discrimination
  Grades 1-12
Active Math
Math Enrichment
  Grades 4-7
Time Tables Challenge
30 Math Games
  PreK-1
Early Skills Series:
  Addition to Five, Counting and
  Recognition to Five, Cutting Activities,
  Early Visual Skills

Spatial Relations
  Grades 1-2, 3-4, 5-6
High Interest Geometry
  Grades 5-8
Money Matters
  Grades 1, 2, 3

LANGUAGE ARTS

Multiple-Choice Comprehension
  Grades 2-3, 4-5, 6-7
My Desktop Dictionary
  Grades 2-5
Spelling Essentials
  Grades 3-10
Reading for Detail
  Grades 4-5, 6-7
Writing Frameworks
  Grades 2-3, 4-5, 6-7
Spelling Success
  Grades 1, 2, 3, 4, 5, 6, 7
My Junior Spelling Journal
  Grades 1-2
My Spelling Journal
  Grades 3-6
Cloze Encounters
  Grades 1-2, 3-4, 5-6
Comprehension Lifters
  1, 2, 3, 4
Grammar Skills
  Grades 2-3, 4-5, 6-8
Vocabulary Development through Dictionary Skills
  Grades 3-4, 5-6, 7-8
Recipes for Readers
  Grades 3-6
Step Up To Comprehension
  Grades 2-3, 4-5, 6-8
Cloze
  Grades 2-3, 4-5, 6-8
Cloze in on Language
  Grades 3-5, 4-6, 5-7, 6-8
Initial Sounds Fold-Ups
Phonic Sound Cards
Early Activity Phonics
Activity Phonics
Early Phonics in Context
Phonics in Context
Build-A-Reader
Communicating
  Grades 5-6
Oral Language
  Grades 2-3, 4-5, 6-8
Listen! Hear!
  Grades 1-2, 3-4, 5-6
Phonic Fold-Ups
Word Study
  Grades 2-3, 4-5, 6-7, 7-8

Draw to a Cloze
  Grades 5-8
Classical Literature
  Grades 3-4, 5-6, 5-8
High Interest Vocabulary
  Grades 5-8
Literacy Lifters
  1, 2, 3, 4
Look! Listen! Think!
  Grades 2-3, 4-5, 6-7
Teach Editing
  Grades 2-3, 3-4, 5-6
Proofreading and Editing
  Grades 3-4, 4-8, 7-8
High Interest Language
  Grades 5-8
Comprehend It!
  Grades 1-3, 4-5, 6-8
Comprehension for Young Readers
Language Skill Boosters
  Grades 1, 2, 3, 4, 5, 6, 7
Phonic Charts
Vocabulary Sleuths
  Grades 5-7, 6-9
Early Theme Series:
  Bears, Creepy Crawlies, The Sea
Phonics in Action Series:
  Initial Sounds, Final Consonant Sounds, Initial Blends and Digraphs, Phonic Pictures

OTHERS

Exploring Change
  Grades 3-4, 5-6, 7-8
Ancient Egypt, Ancient Rome, Ancient Greece
  Grades 4-7
Australian Aboriginal Culture
  Grades 3-4, 5-6, 7-8
Reading Maps
  Grades 2-3, 4-5, 6-8
The Music Book
  Grades 4-8
Mapping Skills
  Grades 2-3, 3-4, 5-6
Introducing The Internet
Internet Theme Series:
  Sea, The Solar System, Endangered Species
Art Media

Visit us at:
www.worldteacherspress.com
for further information and free sample pages.